Translation into English by Christine Grimm

AND NOW?!

ELKE RIESS

authorHOUSE®

AuthorHouse™
1663 Liberty Drive
Bloomington, IN 47403
www.authorhouse.com
Phone: 1-800-839-8640

First published by AuthorHouse 9/13/2011

ISBN: 978-1-4567-9603-7 (e)
ISBN: 978-1-4567-9605-1 (sc)

Library of Congress Control Number: 2011916114

Printed in the United States of America

Stillness is the only thing in the world that has no form. But then, it is not really a thing, and it is not of this world!

CONTENTS

INTRODUCTION

What if the world collapses? Will the prophecies about the end of the world become true? How can we protect ourselves against the catastrophes that are apparently multiplying and becoming more tragic?

Yes, humanity is in a state of distress! People ask me for advice about dealing with the increasing radioactivity. My response is the following: "If you don't know, then who should know?" I can tell you to do anything from hoarding food, practicing certain physical exercises, and taking energy pills to building caves. But this is absurd!

The current problems were created by human beings, so they also carry the solutions within them.

As Albert Einstein already said, "We cannot solve our problems with the same thinking we used when we created them."

And once again, I listen to the inner call to write another book as a reminder to you and to bring some truths to the table.

So is there a solution for the current insanity on this planet? Yes!

It is simpler than you think, but this does not necessarily mean that it is easy.

As I already wrote in my previous books, "You have every conceivable form of support for success!"

The contents of this book cannot be found anywhere else. It is not the first time that someone has written about this topic. People already spoke about it many thousands of years ago.

Once again, this is the moment in which humanity is enlightened about what is really at stake. And this is how I let it happen.

What I write about here is not simply information that you receive every day from the media. Instead, this is about your true being! This is about *you!*

Human beings do not learn from their errors, and

they also do not learn from their suffering. The history of the humanity is evidence of this. We do not make progress with learning here, but we do with remembering!

SOLUTION

It may seem like a very special approach to start a book with the solution—almost like starting with the happy ending and then telling the related story. But this is how it appeared within me, so I followed the instructions. This book does not have a happy *ending* but a happy *being*—forever!

A) Sinking Boat

The momentary state of humanity can best be described as follows: Noah's ark is sinking! On board, there are just human beings because the others have already reached safety. The ocean is raging, the waves are looming high, and the situation is very serious!

What is the solution? What should be done?

What would you do?

- Jump ship and swim? This is hopeless because you will drown. After all, there is no one out there to rescue you.

- Cling to the boat? This means going down with it, which is also an interesting nonsolution.

- Commit suicide? You can also wait to drown because there really is no big difference.

- Pray? I hope that there is a god for you and that this god also has time to listen to you at that moment, let alone rescue you.

- Or choose the following solution? *You are the ocean and the waves!* There is no you *and* the ocean. You are connected with everything and made of the same substance.

As long as you cling to being a human, to suffering, and to being detached from the world and fighting against everything, you will lose. If you continue to use all of your strength to keep yourself separate from the entire creation, you will no longer exist as a human being.

Remind yourself of your true nature, your being, and your part in the oneness, and you will receive all of the hints pointing to the solution.

B) Evolution

This creation is based on evolution. It is an unending, creative process. Everything is constantly in a state of development, change, and transformation, and it is peppered with miracles.

Just think of a few major evolutionary steps: ice ages, climate changes, shifting of the oceans, and continents that have disappeared.

There were dinosaurs, and some transformed themselves to the extent that they are still present in our time in a completely new costume.

And many other living beings and plants have undergone unbelievable developments.

Neanderthals have changed into the human form that is familiar to us now.

The Earth increases its frequencies, shifts the poles,

and changes its magnetic structures, because it is a living being.

Everything is in motion. Everything is in an eternal dance!

And everything is one. Each part is connected with the others and comes from the same source!

This could continue like this forever, and it will, with one exception, the human being!

Human beings have removed, separated, and stopped themselves from participating in this dance.

It is fascinating to look at the overall picture of creation and discover the holography in it. Everything is present in everything else and often infinitely visible within it again.

The human form is what is no longer represented in this picture. Humans have removed themselves from the hologram and simultaneously have the arrogance to think that they have everything under control.

What happened?

At a certain point in time, humans catapulted

themselves out of evolution. This will be discussed in detail in the chapter titled Matrix.

Instead of *being*, they have chosen to *be human*. And they have put their faith in this idea and developed a concept out of it. All of this has become their reality.

Everything is in a constant state of change and evolution. It requires openness, freedom and presence from you in order for the evolution to occur. It happens completely on its own and in a natural way, which is how this entire universe *moves*. This possesses a magic, knowledge, and a power that has no words.

At some point, human beings began to cling to their form. They created a box for themselves and then manifested it. They cling to an idea and concept that are subject to the external appearance of certain laws. In addition, they define the characteristics of beauty and perfection that must be attained. They still identify with this box and believe that this is what being human looks like. This type of separation from the natural flow of evolution mainly brings suffering and disease with it.

What has been lost is the natural development and adaptation to their surrounding world. Humans have become the enemy within their own inner and outer worlds.

They interpret everything that occurs around them as danger, threat, and battle.

The current climate change is a problem for human beings! Instead of accepting the change and adapting to it (even physically), they cling to their form and their box.

From this perspective, they believe that they must control and fight something.

Human beings are becoming increasing allergic to nature! Who is sick here? If you are allergic to your own living space, then you are probably most allergic to yourself! You *are* your surrounding world.

Your inner world is mirrored on the outside—100 percent! If you declare nature as your enemy, you will have some mighty big problems. You will not be able to invent many substances, and there will never be enough protection and defense so that you can move within it. The pharmaceutical business is already earning a fortune on allergies and feels free to advertise this fact.

Wake up! You have become your own worst enemy!

What is momentarily happening on this earth is that humans are destroying themselves. In more precise terms, human beings are destroying being human!

And it really is time for this to happen!

The state of being human has actually been exhausted, and in itself, it is self-destructive. Here is a calming thought for those who are afraid that the Earth will be annihilated: This universe cannot be destroyed by human beings. It has powers and miracles that will always allow it to continue to exist.

This is what will happen: Being human will be eliminated or fade away. What remains is the being!

The current steps of evolution can be described as follows: The Earth has increased its frequency over the past few years, which means that it is turning more quickly. The calculation of time has long been incorrect, and many things move more quickly and are possible now. Manifestations are one example of this.

This frequency produces a new type of creation. Even if it barely exists as a thought, it can already be realized in the outside world at almost the same time. Healing can occur much faster than ever, because the speed in the cells and their division and renewal is accelerated.

Awakening and enlightenment can happen more quickly than ever, because this frequency has a supportive effect on your true being.

Do you even perceive all of this? Or are you so busy with your human dilemma that you overlook what is essential?

What makes you cling so hard to the old familiar stereotypes of the daily, limited existence that you fail to perceive these wonders? And together with the miracles, you also overlook all of the hints, characteristics, and invitations to lead a life in abundance.

The Earth has moved into a neutral magnetic field. A plus and minus field no longer exists. But humans manage to act as if everything has remained the same by believing in this kind of reality and clinging to it. This is a pure illusion and does not correspond with the truth.

What does this mean for you?

If your system exists in a zero frequency, you can choose to wake up and recognize your true being because it is at home in the source of zero magnetism. Or you lose your mind because your human existence can no longer orient itself. And yes, your concept is based on the idea that you are built upon plus and minus poles.

My observations have shown me that 60 percent of the population is currently crazy and 38 percent are desperately "flailing about," not knowing what is happening to them. An entire 2 percent are surrendering to evolution, which means that they are willing to find out who they really are and free themselves from the idea of being human.

This is neither good nor bad: It is what it is! And the direction in which you would like to move and which group you feel drawn to is up to you.

We all have the same starting point and all have this same opportunity for a new experience!

The content of this current phase of evolution is ingenious. It is truly bringing a quantum leap into the events of the moment. You could consider it a gift to be present in such an exciting time and stage of development. You literally have your awakening served to you on a platter!

It is easier than ever and more urgent to know your true being.

Here is what you receive instead your human

identification: pure truthfulness, joy, oneness, abundance, love, almightiness, and freedom!

Everything is always available to you, and you can have completely new experiences without limitations and without a concept.

And do not believe that I am telling you something new. Human beings are also saying that humanity is destroying itself, but in the process, they forget that they identify themselves as human.

The time has come for an awakening!

C) Life Task

Is there a purpose for why you are here? No.

This has nothing to do with purpose, goals, or achieving something. None of this exists. You will truly comprehend this at the latest when you are awakened. And yet, it is something special to be here and have this experience, even though your so-called human experience is only a small portion of this and the essential focus is on your true being. Although this appears to have gotten lost in the development, it is now pushing itself into the foreground with more presence and urgency.

When we appear on this earth, each of us has a life task. The concept of the heart's desire describes it more precisely; however, this is not the desire based on our human identification but the source of the almighty. It is not our idea of what we would like to be or represent and not even what we wish we were.

It is not some illusion or imaginary concept of a certain role in your life. What I am talking about here is the desire from your heart, from your deep connection with everything, from the source of unconditional love!

It is your creation—your contribution that you have brought into this world and made visible through your existence!

What happened?

Human beings have not listened to their hearts for the past two thousand years. They have cut themselves off from their inner source, which is connected with everything. Their activities have been misdirected and dictated, and they have let others control them. To this day, 99.9 percent of the population does work that is in no way related to their beings. They do everyday activities that do not come from their true being and from their heart.

Should we wonder that there is war, hate, frustration, and anger on the earth?

Human beings run under a program of suffering and deficit, relinquish their responsibility, and fill the space in a box.

The good news is that you do not have to continue this way until the end of your life. Every moment is an offer to break out and discover who you really are.

It is comfortable to let other people think for you and make the decisions, even if you simultaneously suffer because of this, feel angry, and say that the others are responsible for your unhappiness.

Yet, this seems like an easier way of being than sitting down, listening to inside yourself, and finding out what you would really like to have happen through you.

In my many years in healing work, I have always heard the same stereotypical sentence: "I don't know what my heart's desire is."

I spent years telling the life task to individual human beings because my abilities also allow me to see their calling.

The result is that no one—not one single

person—has translated this heart's desire into reality, not even with the knowledge of what it really would be!

I no longer tell heart's desires to my clients. Instead, I challenge them to find it out on their own (with my support).

The sentence "I don't know!" has one single, clear, and true translation: I don't want to know!

Humans have a type of arrogance toward awareness, which I also call awareness laziness. This means that they do not really want to take a closer look at themselves.

The moment that you know this, you no longer have any excuses for not turning it into reality.

And there is no such thing as not knowing. You already know everything that is related to you and your existence. Yet, wanting to know requires the path of self-exploration and curiosity.

All humans carry the knowing of their heart's desire, their life tasks, within themselves. Every cell in their DNA strand can be read energetically (psychically).

What is so wonderful about turning it into reality?

You first notice that you do not really need or want to talk about it. You create and do what appears and what you want to do.

You do not need any confirmation about it, and stop asking other people for their opinion on it. You know from a deep source that what you are creating must be exactly like it is.

The result is creations that amaze even you. Without concepts, laws, or learning something in advance, you can create everything with an inner knowledge.

There is a kind of inner guidance when and how something would like to be done or created.

And here comes the *solution*: For whatever still presents itself as a problem, you will be shown solutions that do *not* come from the human corner of understanding but integrate the strength and magnificence from the almighty being.

You will be amazed, and there is no doubt that you will turn these ideas into reality. When you are once again in connection with everything, when you understand and perceive all of the signs, a solution will always exist. New possibilities arise as long as you are open and have no specific ideas about what this should look like.

Tools for discovering your life task include the following:

Write down everything that really gives you joy and what you already liked to do as a small child. Then read through your lines and notice whether there are repetitions or a type of red thread.

What appears often or is similar on the list?

Forget all of your ideas or concepts about what you believe that your heart's desire should be. Just be open to what comes up.

Do not expect that you will see a specific line of work. This is not about the human structure of work and earning money. What I am talking about here is your heart and your true task.

Your life task can be expressed in one to two words: *no* more. Everything else is empty talk that you make up on your own.

You do not have to do anything with this information right away, and it doesn't even need to fit into the human framework at all.

The wonderful thing about your heart's desire is the freedom that it can bring to everything and a deep knowing that arises within you about how you can manifest it.

Why is this type of task so important?

You will experience the almighty power, miracles, endless creativity, and joy through it. In addition, it creates a fulfilled being. You will experience what it means to be in the flow, how you are inwardly guided, and how everything is already there for you.

Furthermore, you make a contribution to this creation that is characterized by love and joy. It is simply an enrichment that you are present here.

None of these creative processes and their results brings destruction, power struggles, greed, and a desire to possess with them. These are creations from the heart that are brought in with awareness and clarity. They do not have any of the human "craziness" in them.

Of the human inventions, works, and creations that currently exist on the planet, 94 percent are detached from the heart. Instead of supporting life, they burden our existence. Only 6 percent are truly created from the heart, from the source of being. What surrounds you and the things that you pay attention to every day are separated from the being in oneness in their structure and energy. The resulting pile of garbage and surrounding world problems speak for themselves.

What you need is courage! It may be that your task does not allow itself to be pressed into a form. It wants to be designed from within itself and be free. Turn off this boring mental loop. You may say, "Yes, but I need to earn money."

This is the greatest illusion and obstacle that humans have created for themselves. First, the entire money market is already collapsing, and this loop only serves as an excuse to not go deeper and deal with your heart.

As I mentioned above, it is *your* decision whether you recognize yourself, question yourself, and take leave from the identification.

The moment for this is *now!*

D) Eradication of Human Beings

Are you concerned about the outcome of all this? What will be the solution for the drama in this world?

You can sit comfortably on your sofa with more or less stress (even though food, alcohol, cigarettes, TV, and the computer can produce some diversion) and become annoyed about the state of the world.

All human beings do this! They all get agitated and look for the enemy and guilty parties in the outside world. If necessary, the environmental catastrophes also fit the bill here. But is this really the case?

How many tsunamis, earthquakes, and tornados have not already been the creations of human thinking? Because of my ability of clairvoyance, nothing remains hidden from me, and I can very precisely describe for what reason and where everything originates. Some people may be amazed to learn how many powers human beings have.

So whatever happens in the outside world, it is your inner world that is happening on the outside. Your battles, hatred, and despair are so destructive.

And, once again, there is a solution:

Humans are destroying themselves—quite simply and quickly! The human identification, this strange type of mutation, is eradicating itself.

Wonderful!

Because they are not integrated into the whole but stubbornly cling to their special role, they are kicking themselves out of the entire picture. Is this sad, terrible, or tragic? No, it is what it is, and it is a completely natural process of selection. It is just too bad if you know about the solution.

Human beings have had such a large amount of time to get to know themselves. Time and again, they have been shaken up, and offers for awakening were presented to them; however, they have become amazingly resistant in their box.

Your true being cannot and will not be eradicated. This is not even possible.

It is only the illusion of being human that disappears sooner or later. You can no longer sit on your sofa and act as if the catastrophes were outside. You *are* the catastrophe!

I know that this is not especially pleasant to read, and you may want to slam the book shut at this point.

The wonderful news is that this is not *you!* This is only the idea of the human being who has come to an end. The entire concept of human is eliminating itself because it no longer permits any more development. It does not help to become a better human being, to be more environmentally conscious and a bit more content. Human beings have developed into a grandiose foreign body within their own world.

The only solution (at the risk of repeating myself) is *your true being!* Wake up! You will be astonished by the beauty, strength, and love that are embedded within you.

Destroy the world? No, this creation is much too inventive and powerful.

The earth does not need to be healed. It radiates, and it *is*. But human beings urgently need to heal themselves in order to know who they truly are.

For example, I was in an area where a giant fire in the mountains had burned the forests. A few years later, I hiked through an ocean of flowers and plants, a paradise with wonderful trees.

The earth draws on its unending creative force. This planet is connected with its heart task, which means that it is flexible, open, free, and almighty.

Do not worry about the outside world, but use every moment to know yourself. Because of your awakening, the outside world will heal itself through your being.

E) Learning

Is there something to learn? No.

You must remember! What is unavoidable here is the homework, which I extensively described in my first few books.

However, this homework does not serve to help you know more or pass an exam. There is no information or knowing in the human sense. Instead, this is pure self-exploration, looking in the mirror and going more deeply within yourself.

Nothing of what the human being learns makes sense. In the schools, universities, and vocational training, knowledge is just lectured on so that it can be repeated seamlessly and without reflecting on it. So what is creative and essential about that?

Some of you will also protest at this point. Okay, after you have become agitated about this—as is the case with most human beings—sit back down and please give my sentence some precise consideration.

Your being does not need to learn anything. It knows what it needs! Just like the animals, human beings learn the essential things by imitating them. Anything else that allows humans to be different than the animal world is not learned but experienced through dedication and listening.

The difference is that human nature has the strength and consciousness for creating. It can create something *new*.

All of the learning from prefabricated structures, laws, principles, rules, and knowledge from the past is senseless. None of this is true. None of this contributes to your being, and none of it makes your life easier or more fulfilled.

And some of you are already groaning, "But what about writing and reading?"

Here is a story on this topic: A team of highly respected professors and scientists traveled to the reservations of Indian tribes so they could have conversations with them. The Western world wanted to exchange thoughts with these native peoples.

The elders of the Indian tribes and the Western group sat together at the campfire. The professors began to ask their questions on the first evening. After the Indians discussed them a bit with each other, the group was dispatched with just one brief sentence.

Somewhat dissatisfied, the scientists launched

another attempt at communication the next day, but this was no more successful than the one on the previous day. On the third day, one of the important professors became exasperated. With an air of indignation, he asked the Indian elder what this meant. They had travelled so far just to talk and exchange ideas, and the only thing that they had experienced was a lack of answers.

At this point, the eldest turned to him and said, "How can we exchange thoughts with each other if you cannot share the silence with us. You will experience everything that we could tell you in it."

Are words necessary?

At the moment when children learn how to talk and become immersed in the language, the separation from their true being occurs.

What happened to me? When I now want to speak slowly, I cannot talk anymore! I need a certain speed before I can communicate through the language. Have I become dumb, sick, or crazy?

No, this is truthfulness! This is when speech becomes silent because everything has been said and there is nothing more to explain.

Pure being, being in the now, does not have and does not need any words.

In the so-called ancient cultures, there was no writing. They communicated through signs.

Where did they disappear to? Nowhere! They were in a perfect connection with being, appearing and leaving in the natural evolution. Their creation came from the power of the heart. This is why people are now astonished about the archeological finds and have many questions about how these structures were possible.

How? Quite simply, they were created from the almighty power—without limitation, without the law of gravity, and without physical formulas. The wonders emerged from a deep knowing and the freedom of letting it happen.

No doctrine of beliefs and no human concepts stood in the way.

You are from the same being as these peoples of the high cultures. You are boundless and almighty.

There is nothing to learn here. This is about having experiences—in joy and with astonishment!

If you really desire to have information, the

Internet now exists, and it's filled with concepts, programs, and human structure!

But what you will miss is the moment that gives you all of the signs and teaches you everything about what is now essential for your existence.

You may have learned much, but you no longer understand the world!

Isn't this crazy? Rational knowledge adds nothing and has no connecting point with your true core. Just listening, being still, and having awareness allows you to comprehend this world and be a part of it.

An individual can hardly go out into nature these days without immediately needing another person as protection. Isn't this innately grotesque?

But when you go out into nature in the experience of your true being, you simultaneously are nature! What happens here has no words. It is pure joy and connectedness.

Science suspects that everything is connected with everything else. Scientists research with the methods that they have learned in prefabricated structures and instructions in order to get to the bottom of things. It is absurd to approach being in oneness in this manner. This almighty creation cannot be understood and comprehended with the rational mind. You must let yourself fall into the being, into the being in oneness. You must *be* it. Then you will know everything, and there is also nothing more to know.

Can you learn this? No, you must experience it! No teacher can explain it to you. My task is simply to remind you of it and shake up all of your cells with my being.

This may seem like it is strenuous and tiring to you. When you are with me, your entire human cell system will go into a state of resistance, which will let you become exhausted and aggressive. But if you do not pay too much attention to all of this, the power of your true being will become stronger and stronger. And you will want more of this, because it gives you a taste of your wonderful essence.

F) Completely Supported

What happens to you and what you allow to happen to you is your free choice. It is up to you to discover your true being or to insist that you are a human being.

It is already very telling that the importance of

giving a name to everything completely vanishes with enlightenment. Everything is what it is. Does it require a term or categorization? None of this occurs. You perceive what is without any evaluations, judgments, and names.

The human being as such also falls under the table with this.

What is so different when you are no longer human? Does it mean that you will be destroyed and annihilated by your own race?

No, it doesn't. On the one hand, you no longer exist as such, and this type of illusion vanishes as a result. On the other hand, you will receive all of the information that allows you to continue being here. Apart from this, it will become more than clear to you that there is neither birth nor death and that everything is pure being.

In this being and on your journey of discovery to yourself, you will notice major changes in your awareness and perception. An appreciation of everything that appears in this universe develops completely on its own. This is not just talking about the connection with everything. Instead, you will have the personal experience of being one with this world.

Because of this connectedness, you will develop a completely new consciousness of how you treat yourself on the inside and outside. You will perceive the beauty and magnificence of this creation and automatically desire to serve it.

At the same time, your so-called outer world is interested in supporting and carrying you.

How is this manifested in the present moment?

The Earth has raised its frequency, which may make it easier for you to once again experience yourself as a multidimensional being. This means that you are not only present in your familiar physical form but that you also mirror yourself in multiple ways. Once again, this brings us back to the hologram. Everything is represented in everything else and in infinite multiples.

At the same time, your level of perception is not only oriented upon the idea of a three-dimensional world. You grasp everything that is happening but do not need any consciousness to put it into words and linear thoughts. Without speaking about it and needing to filter it, a certain knowledge is present.

This results in an unbelievable speed in translating the ideas and creations into reality. This allows you to simultaneously grasp a number of inputs and hold them in your mind.

The thought and action structure of the human level has been brutally slowed at this time. People think, create, and act in a linear form. First comes A and then B and then C.

This is not the natural level of being, which is distinguished by the present moment—the perception and reception of everything that is right now. This means that the sluggish concept of the past and future ceases because they are no longer present. As a result, the entire storage capacity is ready for the now.

As already mentioned above, the Earth has transformed itself into a zero magnetic field on the subtle level. This automatically supports your awakening, because it silences the areas of your brain that are responsible for the neurotic chatter. These areas are turned off on the energetic level. It has been possible up to now for you to experience this in nature. It creates a vibrational pattern (synthropic field) that helps you become still and brings you into contact with your being.

The entire creation is now in this state, which makes it easier for you to find yourself.

Another aid to help you join in the current evolution is transformation of the entire earth. All living beings, every plant, and anything that is present at this moment is the carrier of the same DNA. This will be explained in greater detail in the Matrix chapter. Our double helix, which is represented in every cell, has changed energetically in recent years. An activation of twelve strands instead of just two has occurred. These have always been present but not visible. They are light strands.

Their task is to experience us anew in our almightiness. It is a wonderful expansion of the boundless possibilities of our existence. This is simultaneously involved with an evolutionary step that is transforming the entire planet into a light being.

How much support do you still need? Everything is ready.

However, as long as you insist upon your separation and only pace back and forth in your box, you will not be able to make contact with all of this because you are actually fighting with every bit of strength against these offers.

Let yourself be supported! All of this development has such a fascinating knowledge and love in the form of its realization that you can truly trust in it. Nothing and no one is interested in your suffering and demise. This destruction is solely your product. Clinging to your identification as one person is no longer tenable. It is now outdated. The idea of the human being is exhausted and leads nowhere. There is no naturalness, no evolution, and no further development in being human.

Your being is not touched by this. It is always present. You will experience your natural calling in it.

G) Comfort Zone

It is astonishing how comfortable the unpleasant and miserable experiences can be. Human beings have made themselves at home in this state and are now hoping for the redeemer.

The important thing is that this is not the final state. The experience of being human is a small portion of the unending repertoire of being. But if you believe that this is the only reality, it becomes a fixed idea. Then you think that this is all that can be experienced here on earth.

Human beings assume that there is something like a universal fear and that this creation has already stored it in its memory. I can only give you one word of advice on this: Please wake up and recognize your being. Then this nonsense about your assumptions and research will stop!

Nothing is stored on the universal level, especially not emotion. The only power field upon which this entire creation is built is that of love. And once again, this is not about the human concept of love but the true, unconditional love. If this did not exist, human beings would have stopped existing a long time ago in this form. But because everything originates in it, the creation does not let anyone be left behind in this sense.

Even the current development of humanity extinguishing itself is ingenious. This does not refer to an end-of-the-world mood, drama, or anything terrible. After all, you can immediately experience who you really are at any time. This is just how everything that has shut itself off from love and true creation is eliminated. At the same time, this occurrence shakes you to move forward with the awakening on both the outside and inside.

Your experience is not reduced to being human. This is actually just the introduction. It is intended to make you curious about your true being. And one idea of this is suffering, deficit, and limitation. Instead of getting comfortable with it, this should motivate you to get out of it and acknowledge it.

Fear is certainly an essential factor in your comfort zone. Apart from the fact that it is only invented and fed every day by each human being, fear only occurs when you wander into the future. As long as you are in the here and now, it does not exist. Yet, this emotion is already so deeply anchored that human beings assume it is a natural component.

Why am I focusing on fear at this point? Because it is the most intrusive companion when you try to free yourself from the identification as a human being. It lurks in a thousand faces during your self-exploration. Its main task is to make things so miserable for you that you are glad to get cozy in the comfort zone again. Please do not forget that it is a phantom! Pay no attention to it, and it will disappear on its own.

Don't make excuses to yourself with these words: "After all, I'm afraid."

Don't make it so simple for yourself. Look at what is behind this simple sentence.

Another comfortable pillow in your box that you can lean on is your belief.

You do not find solutions by believing in something. Solutions are created from the deep almighty knowledge. Pay attention to how often you use the words "I believe" (which constitutes a large portion of the vocabulary on all of the continents that I have already travelled to) in your sentences. Do you believe, or do you know?

Do not hide behind your belief but examine what you really know. It may be that not much remains of knowledge, but this is not what is actually important here. The essential thing is your truthfulness. You know something from your own experience, but this is also just knowledge in relation to *your* experience. This cannot be developed into a concept or a rule. It simultaneously contains an unbelievable freedom: Nothing requires an explanation or a form. You experience everything as pure and new in your being.

The human comfort zone no longer has a solution for the current dilemma. The researchers can search until the cows come home. Spiritual perceptions are available in the marketplace, and increasingly more information is published with the great assumption that there probably is something like being in oneness.

It is no longer appropriate to ponder about this and make assumptions.

Actions are needed!

The solutions are all there—simple, tangible, and wonderful! But you will only be able to see and experience them in your own being, not as a human being.

> *Time is not at all what it appears to be.*
> *It does not flow just in one direction,*
> *and the future exists simultaneously*
> *with the past.*

> —Albert Einstein, Physicist

MATRIX

What does this term mean?

One translation of it is "crystalline grid network."

What image does this present to you? It is simply the idea of storing information in a crystal. In energetic terms, it is depicted as a grid in which certain codes are present. These can be deleted and stored anew at any time.

Such a matrix holds enormous power because it determines the entire world of experiences for human beings.

A) Human Matrix

The term matrix has increasingly popped up during the past few years, especially in correlation with the idea of being in oneness. It is based on the assumption that there is something like a creation matrix in which the entire universe—together with everything that belongs to it—is represented.

The so-called human existence is stored here. But an additional matrix has formed for human beings during the course of their development, one that has separated itself from the all-encompassing grid network.

The matrix has been covered with the information of deficit and suffering through the genetic code. A world of experience has been created for human beings through this grid network that involves battles, a lack of self-esteem, duality, envy, and hate. All of this has allowed it to turn into reality.

The good news is that human beings are not forced to remain in this form and information until the end of their lives. And yet, this is the perspective from which people observe the world at this time.

The most essential point in this entire development is that there is no longer any further development within this matrix. The result is that humanity's level of experience is trapped within itself. The illusion that this is going somewhere may prevail, but a look at world events reflects an end point in a simple and clear way.

Humans are just focused on themselves, and none of the new paths of consciousness, spiritual perceptions, and research results leads to a change, especially not to a loving, creative world of experience.

There might be a great deal of talk about how we could rescue this planet and which prayers, peace marches, or protests could make any type of insight possible. But none of this is really trailblazing.

The reason for this is not because human beings do not want to actually try it. Instead, they are not aware of their own program and do not search to find their true core.

Otherwise, the scales would have already fallen from their eyes long ago, and they would have realized that their efforts within the human matrix may be nice but do not really contain a solution for the actual issue here.

Many wonderful masters and philosophers have pointed out time and again that your true being and your magnificence are hidden deep within you. This is where you get in touch with highest wisdom and receive every solution.

But reading and listening is not enough in this case. You must experience it for yourself.

Even now it is also the only path into freedom, love, and healing.

This healing begins with you and automatically affects everything that surrounds you.

What exactly does the human matrix involve?

Each human cell contains a two-meter-long strand of DNA in the form of a double helix. Researchers have discovered and developed the concept that twenty-three pairs of chromosomes are responsible for the human genetic code.

These are apparently responsible for the appearance and feelings on the physical and psychic level— and even for being human.

Scientists have never been able to decode the rest of this strand, so they consider it garbage. This will be discussed in detail below.

In any case, a matrix has laid itself over this package of chromosome pairs like a veil. This means that the stored information has gradually defined the state of being human.

Humanity then selects its definition and identification from this energetic file. If we look at the entire world, this is always reduced to the same attitudes, belief systems, and actions.

This is like a certain repertoire that is lived by generation after generation. It is obviously possible to make excuses by saying that this is how humans are (and an astonishing number of people actually do this). But this is difficult to reconcile when it is simultaneously apparent that human beings are endowed with unbelievable powers, a brain, consciousness, creativity, and possibilities that somehow are hardly given a chance to develop.

This DNA is present in everything in a wondrous way. The double helix is not only found in human beings but in the entire creation.

Everything in this universe has this same starting basis, which serves as the simplest evidence that it is really connected with everything else. But what may be simple within nature is confined in human beings because of the limited information.

It is like a box that has been placed over th genetic code.

Within this coded matrix, there are probably thousands of variations, suggesting that being human is in diverse. But a closer look reveals that each of them always have the same components in their story: wanting to be seen, envy, frustration, wanting to possess, lies, deficit, hate, suffering, hardship, fear, doubt, and the longing for love.

What determines the true being in the form of the human body has probably always been present but not activated. In its connection and abundance of almighty information, the DNA remains idle.

At the moment in which you open and explore yourself, some of these programs will already be deleted from this matrix.

When awakening or enlightenment occurs, nothing is left of this human matrix. What remains is the genetic code and complete activation of the DNA strands. This results in the experience of being perfectly connected. You *are* suddenly integrated back into the whole, and the illusion of separation disappears.

In order to facilitate and accelerate the removal of the human matrix, I have published a book with

pictures and exercises to support you on your path to becoming free and realizing your true being, namely *Being Free: 38 Pictures and Exercises to Wake You Up and Set You Free.*

This book describes the thirty-eight basic elements of your almighty matrix that are just waiting to be reactivated. There are also more details about this in the chapter on the thirty-eight ingredients of being.

In this context, it is interesting to not only look at the DNA in the cells but also the cell itself.

The cell membrane in human beings stores all of the attitudes, belief systems, and emotional garbage. Above all, this layer diminishes the permeability of the cell for water, light, and nutrients. All substances that penetrate the cell wall receive coloration from your way of living and thinking. This is a simple way to describe how the cells become diseased.

Within the cell is a cell nucleus that has nothing more to do than continuously divide itself and do so with the information that is present in the cell.

This means that if the cell is responsible for the liver, it will carry this coding within itself. But

if it is bathed in the information soup (attitudes, religious doctrines, etc.), then its statement is the following: I hate the world. Then this cell division will already produce diseased cells.

This also explains why some human beings remain ill despite the power of cell division and renewal. Cleansing and clarification on deeper levels is required for the information to be "healthy."

In addition, each cell also has a silicea chip within it that vibrates continuously and keeps the cell in movement as a result. At the same time, this movement is the life energy or frequency. Researchers puzzle over the location of the charging station for this chip, which sets it in vibration. This involves the true source of creation. Its engine is fed from the ether and kept alive through the frequency of love.

When a person dies, this chip stops vibrating.

As a result, the cell nucleus is not responsible for the life of the cell but for this silicea chip.

Each cell also contains the thirty-eight ingredients, as already mentioned above. These include awareness, magnificence, love, abundance, miracle, and power, just to mention a few. They are the building materials of almighty being.

But since the entire focus and concentration has been placed on the human matrix, the true content seems to be in a state of slumber.

This means that human beings have limited themselves to 0.1 percent of their true strength and possibilities. Yet, it is astonishing what they achieve with just this level of energy.

At the moment in which you awaken, the human matrix disappears, and the entire DNA is accessible in its original state. Interestingly enough, being enlightened does not mean that the almighty force has been activated. It is probably present but not yet in use because every type of identification is dissolved with the awakening and you are completely connected with everything. You experience yourself as a part of the whole and are simultaneously the whole.

What can additionally be integrated into this type of existence is the great potential of the almighty.

The matrix of this creation is fundamentally built upon the energy structures of rose quartz, crystal quartz, and amethyst. On the one hand, this is because these gemstones carry a very specific network structure that stores and directs light in a special way. On the other hand, they are the easiest to program.

They exist within the almighty matrix with no programming whatsoever, but they are in the purest form. In a natural way, rose quartz carries the information of creativity and love. Crystal quartz offers clarity and taking yourself seriously. Amethyst promotes awareness and deep consciousness.

Therefore, these three crystal network structures contain the essential basic foundation for your being, even though the use of words and explanations can never express what this really means. But I am writing about it to at least give you an idea of what you are carrying within you.

B) Almighty Matrix

Everything that you can perceive and observe is built upon the same basic structure. The entire creation consists of a grand "source of information"—at least this is how it seems. Everything is connected with everything else and related at the same time.

As already mentioned in the "Human Matrix"

section, every type of manifestation possesses this same DNA. Apart from the pairs of chromosomes, which represent a type of blueprint for the respective form of creation, they all mirror the same matrix.

At the moment in which you experience enlightenment, this unity with everything is present. This does not mean that it did not previously exist. But because of the human identification, you believe in separation and also experience it as such. You think that you are an individual and there is a world out there, but you are the world: There is no difference between the inside and the outside.

I can see the DNA strands of the plants, animals, stones, planets, etc., with my clairvoyant ability. They all look like ours. This is why I experience my existence without a sense of separation. I *am* a stone, a flower, and everything that appears. As a result, I am also in communication with everything *and* can receive information, guidance, and answers.

The solutions are in and around me. Shamans use various types of natural drugs in order to see the DNA of the plants and then create the necessary remedies. They are given all of the information about how much of each substance is required.

Human beings have so unbelievably restricted themselves in their ways of perceiving and looking at things that they cannot absorb this connectedness and the power of the true creation.

The true matrix holds everything inside within it that can be known and experienced in this existence. But human beings look at the DNA strands from the small perspective of their box and also experiment with them in a crazy way.

They do not even understand precisely what this genetic code—let alone the rest of the strands—contains, and they presume to dig around in them. What a grotesque idea—creating a perfect human being! And this brings us back to our dilemma again.

Instead of allowing an evolution in a natural way through this creation, they cling to an ideal of beauty that is pure illusion.

So what do these DNA strands actually mean?

I am writing here about something that no one has discovered up to now because it is not visible through the human, conceptual way of looking at things.

You see what you are accustomed to seeing and what you expect to see! This is the human, limited approach to its creation! But it is no longer adequate for what surrounds you on both the inside and the outside.

For the past few years, it has been my task to perceive and be able to name *everything*, even though it sometimes takes a while until a word has formed for some things.

As already described under the "Human Matrix," science assumes that the genetic code for human beings consists of twenty-three pairs of chromosomes. This is not really true. There are a total of thirty-two pairs, of which the additional nine pairs are based on light structures that the human's "blocked" eye does not perceive. But not seeing them does not mean that they are nonexistent.

This reminds me once again of Albert Einstein, who communicated this in such a refreshing and wise way: "Whatever we find out about the physical laws, it may be that none of them are really the truth." (He was more than aware of the illusion and limitedness of human thinking.)

The content of these nine chromosome pairs is also designed somewhat differently than those that are familiar to human beings.

They have the following energetic content:

1. Perspective
2. Knowing
3. Generosity
4. Sharing
5. Being one
6. Thankfulness (in relation to the creation)
7. Creativity
8. Taking yourself seriously
9. Awareness

I am not writing this based on some type of esoteric whim but from the source of truthfulness. I would like to add something here that I already discussed in my first book, *Everything Is*. I have experienced a change that allows me to speak only words that comes from the source of the almighty. Nothing else is possible for me.

This means that the mentioning of the nine pairs is not some cute invention. Even I am astonished at their contents because they actually shine a different light on the true human manifestation than human beings are experiencing at the moment.

These are probably present but inactive in any case because the concept of the human is exclusively focused on the so-called researched pairs of chromosomes.

After all, there is still a portion of the DNA that the researchers allow to fall under the table through their ignorance. And the secret that defines the almighty is found right here. This area of the DNA has the most wonderful light bands with codes, but this is not the light frequency that human beings have discovered and set in a formula. They probably already have the variables for it, but the signs for the computation are missing.

Human beings will also not receive this possibility because their brain structure and their box cannot comprehend it. This requires being awakened and opening up all of the senses. This is not present in the linear form of thought. You need 100 percent of your brain capacity and openness to access this information.

But a formula or evidence is not necessary for you on the human level. What is essential is that this light is also present in everything. And what is far more significant is that this light structure constitutes the ether.

What holds things together has always been a major puzzle for human beings. What is between the atoms and molecules? What is it that is actually nothing yet still appears to be something? What is this nothing and something?

The Greeks called it ether, and this is the term that I would like to adopt. The almighty matrix builds itself on a wonderful, special light that cannot be measured and is not visible for the concept and the illusion of human beings.

This light does not consist of a frequency and is not built upon waves.

It is depicted in thousands of pictures with the saints—the halo! Something that these special human beings radiated has been made visible. They were simply connected and activated in the almighty, which made it possible for this light to radiate through them.

This light exists in every human being. These were not and are not special cases. They just no longer identified with being human.

In addition, this also shows in a very plausible way why the evolution of human manifestation moves in the direction of light being. It is its pure nature and it's time to experience this creation as being in the quality of light.

These light strands also exist in everything that is part of the creation. This is probably also why human beings feel so good when they go out into nature (and above all, when they become silent).

This is where you bathe in the wonderful, almighty matrix! The effect is like charging your battery.

Another unbelievable phenomenon is that this light has a type of mirror neuron in it, although human beings also have no access to it as long as they view the world based on their concepts.

I find this very fascinating, for it almost forces humanity to give up its idea about itself because everything that it would like to experience and comprehend cannot be observed from this perspective.

This means that being human must truly make a quantum leap from its illusory box. And everything has already been prepared for this transition.

These mirror neurons are ingenious in their own way. Science has already discovered that the following occurs with these neurons: Another person does something, and this simultaneously triggers the same action in you.

The cause is not related to time and space. This explains why people are amazed at the possibilities suggested by the research that shows how something occurring on one side of the globe can simultaneously take place on the other side.

This solves the puzzle about the speed of transmission and the source of information transport. This type of light is beyond human measurement, and the mirror neurons are present holographically. There is no start and no end, no now and then.

Only this moment is present, and *everything* is in it.

Here is something else that may astonish you: Scientists believe that prayers, feelings, emotions, and thoughts can have an effect on the earth. Although this is true, it is interesting to note that this is not related to the ether, the means of transport, or the mirror neurons. The level of your inner, human world that is shown on the outside is solely transported on the vibrational level of the morphogenetic fields.

These fields are creations from the human

existence and programmed with the human forms of appearance.

Everything that is related to the natural, almighty evolution is distributed and visible through the light source and mirror neurons.

Every conceptual human idea and identification chooses the self-created, morphogenetic fields as its vehicle. They store everything that manifests in the human form. This is where human beings draw their worlds of feelings, emotions, and thoughts, which they then declare as their own.

You can also download your abilities from other human beings, but they still come from the box of your identification.

When you awaken and no longer exist as a human being, these morphogenetic fields expire. Then your being is connected to the almighty. Then the creation matrix is 100 percent present within you. Each cell is awakened and radiates. And then it is your decision whether to actively integrate them or not.

I would like to delve more precisely into the almighty matrix in relation to human beings.

As already described above, a special matrix within the almighty grid network always builds upon the three gemstone structures of rose quartz, crystal quartz, and amethyst.

The crystal quartz assumes your form of manifestation. The rose quartz serves your heart's desire. And the amethyst is purest awareness in this process.

The form of manifestation is an octagonal star in which your being centers itself. This form has been reduced to pentagonal stars. A famous example of this is the picture by Leonardo da Vinci in which a human being is drawn within the five-point star.

So that box is already here! I have nothing against the master Leonardo da Vinci. He was a genius, and he worked for the church!

Unconscious programs let him alienate the true form. If the eight-point star carries a balanced cross within it, this orientation no longer exists in the five-point star.

Instead of the isosceles cross, the sign of suffering (Christ's cross) was used here. It is astonishing how this symbol of suffering and its associated history have created the deepest programs.

When I look into the human matrix, I find it astounding that all human beings who work for other human beings also suffer unconsciously for them according to the motto "If I help, then I must suffer."

I am not just simply writing this. It is a fact in human existence. It is up to you to examine this carefully and stop doing the suffering.

When you recognize your true being, you will find yourself smiling many times about all of the things that actually never existed yet had still previously determined your so-called life.

You *are not* twenty-three pairs of chromosomes and a human matrix.

Your being is embedded in the matrix of the almighty creation! Wake up and surf in the truthful evolution!

> *Science cannot decipher the mystery*
> *of nature. And this is the case because*
> *we ourselves are a part of this mystery*
> *that we are attempting to decipher.*
>
> —Max Planck, Physicist

BEING AND NOW

Being and the now are not separable from each other. The one automatically contains the other. When you are in the moment, there is perfect presence and immediacy. There is no person, no thinking, and no controlling in this state.

It is so simple, yet it appears so difficult to attain this from the human level. It may not be possible to achieve being in the now because you are already in the present. Instead, this involves devoting yourself to being still and letting everything pass through you.

In this type of permeability, you are told, shown, and presented with everything that is essential for you. Everything that requires a solution will be revealed to you, and you will be given clues.

Being human is based on this concept: We learn through suffering.

This statement can hardly be accurate. No one has ever learned through suffering. If this were true, everyone would already be enlightened here and in a state of pure, true being. Considering the extent of suffering that already has existed and still exists on earth, every human being would place the highest priority on exploring him or herself and escaping from this misery.

But this philosophy has not changed anything for the better. Instead, it has given rise to strategies of suffering and comfort zones but had not given any pressure to think about things and go any deeper.

The current world events are at least as horrible as those that occurred many hundreds of years ago. This reminds me of a lecture by Krishnamurti, an Indian philosopher, who could not comprehend why humanity did not learn from its wars.

The answer is that the human matrix contains no solution for this problem. Instead, the earth is engaged in the Third World War and has failed to even "notice" it. Japan has learned nothing from Hiroshima (and neither has the rest of the world). Nuclear reactors are no longer under control and lead to massive radioactivity on our planet. So-called epidemics appear, and somehow, it is not possible to find the causes. But assumptions that create waves are put forward each time.

Most foods are treated with antibiotics, which is a perfect model for weakening the human organism. Vaccinations have become mandatory for childhood diseases, which are normally the basis for developing the immune system.

I could continue this list infinitely. It is not necessary to fight wars with weapons, but this is done incessantly.

Human beings are eliminating themselves in the quickest possible way.

As strange as it may sound, even this is perfect! Humanity creates a scenario from within itself that perhaps creates so much fear and worry that each individual seeks a way out.

The only solution to be free and step back into the oneness is you true being.

Do not waste any energy in resisting the above lines. This is not about expressing your opinion about them.

First, explore what I have written here. First,

scrutinize your person, your own manifestation, and then consider the content one more time.

Until you have begun to truly look at yourself in the mirror, every type of concept and statement about yourself is moot. And I am very serious about this!

This is not just a bit of talk about being and now and adding some senseless jargon to it.

I am not writing from the experience of a wishy-washy spiritual state of being. Instead, everything that I share with you serves to remind you of your magnificent being and comes from the purest, truest experience and knowledge.

This is an offer for you to open up to yourself deeper and deeper so that you will be able to encounter what humanity has created in an open and almighty way.

A) Pendulum

As a human being, you experience your existence with highs and lows, happiness and unhappiness, and positive and negative occurrences. Everything is labeled and evaluated. In this apparently constant movement, you set out in search of your center and balance. There are a multitude of available offers that want to help you in this process.

Some of these may accomplish more or less— that is, until you get into a stress situation, and it catapults you back into the old behavior patterns.

I would like to use the image of a pendulum to describe this: Being human is like swinging from one side to the other like a pendulum. The exciting factor is that it must pass through the center each time. This offers the possibility of once again remembering what it means to be in balance. Yet, human existence contains the concept of duality, so it creates an energetic field that pushes and pulls you back and forth.

When you hear the statements made by human beings, this idea becomes increasingly reinforced. If you are moving too much in one direction, you must automatically be forced to also experience the other side.

Is this really how it is? Or is this a creation of the human matrix? You may hear something like the following: "You cannot just be happy. When you have experienced a high phase, a low will certainly follow!" Is this true?

What occurs with this pendulum in being? It hangs straight down like a plumb. At the same time, it is also awake in this silence.

It notices the pushing and pulling in all directions, but it does not go along with it!

It observes these fields without participating in them. Sometimes a type of exhaustion occurs when this wrangling lasts too long, not because of resistance against going along with it but because of the exhaustion of observing these forces.

The pendulum comes to rest when you no longer cling to being human. At the same time, this means that you no longer let yourself be determined by the emotional, neurotic world or by the stories.

Some may think that life will then become boring because they perceive and identify through these extremes; however, this is pure drama and definitely very exhausting.

What is so special about this resting pendulum? It contains both the repose and the presence. In addition, it allows you to be present and attentive in all directions because you are not occupied with swinging in one certain direction. And should it become really important for you to be in a frequency, you are open and prepared for it at all times.

It is a completely different experience of your existence in this reality. Drama no longer has any space here. But this is precisely what some human beings appear to consider as their elixir of life. This is what psychotherapies see as the manic and depressive phase.

There is no center because off-center no longer exists. Your being *is!* I do not experience inner balance because it is simpler. These concepts become completely irrelevant. When you are connected with everything and fed by the light of almighty strength, no extra exercises are required. And yet, silence and listening provide support in experiencing this resting pendulum. When you are in a state of awareness and gratitude, it is simply there.

B) Heart Connection

"You must connect with your heart and listen to your heartbeat. Then you can speak with them." This is a sentence from the wonderful film *Avatar*. The beings on its planet are connected with nature and the animal world, with which they communicate. When they open up to the heartbeat of the creation, it serves them.

You only need to say farewell to your separateness and enter into being in oneness. Everything speaks and communicates through the heart.

"I see *you*," says the creature to the human being and looks into his eyes. This is also a beautiful sentence from the film. True seeing is meant here, the true knowing of "I know who you are really."

"It is only with the heart that one can see rightly. What is essential is invisible to the eye." This sentence from the book *The Little Prince* is based on the same perception.

I experience my seeing through heart. I do not need to open my eyes in order to see. My clairvoyance does not use the physical eye. It is an inner seeing. Everything is revealed through the heart and is sent in pictures, words, and so forth.

All enlightened people have open seeing: They see you—your being! This determines their existence in exactly the same way. And this is where love is.

You look in the mirror and believe that you are the person who is looking back at you. But you see through eyes that only perceive certain portions, and these are already overlaid with projections, information, and programs.

When you awaken and your person no longer exists, then you see what actually is. And this *is* simple—without any text, evaluation, or correction. The form disappears, and there is no longer any fitting into something else.

Based on this being, each of us has a type of heart task. I also use the term heart's desire, although the desire is not related to the individual but to the creation. This task is visible to my eyes in everyone's DNA strands. The code is written there. A better way to express it is that your task is reflected in the strands.

So why is a task necessary here if there is no goal and no achievement?

This heart's desire allows you to have an experience in abundance, endless creativity, joy, the strength of productivity, and love. You make a contribution that lets this creation become even more radiant. The almighty potential can become visible through you. You experience a boundless flow and presence.

I am astonished by the diversity and ingenious

ideas of this creation. Absolutely nothing is missing. If you set out on the path to find out who you truly are, this task will be revealed to you. Each of us has his own access to it. Even if so many people say, "I don't know what my task is," my only response to this is the following: "Then find out. You have already received all of the information about it that you need."

My experience has shown me that it does not help for me to tell you what your heart's desire is. Even if I do, this does not mean that you will turn it into reality. Your effort is truly required to find it out, and then it is still your free choice to follow it or not.

And the universe will make everything available to you so that you can turn it into reality.

What happens during this task of the heart is unbelievable. Your person and your entire manifestation shifts into the background when you begin to follow it.

You are in the now, without time and space. And you will experience what there is to do from this source.

C) Eye

When I write about being and now, the eye comes to mind and needs to be mentioned.

What exactly happens with the eyes is not clear to science and medicine to this day. They suspect that this sense may still conceal many secrets.

We use our eyes to see. But what? Human beings see what they are accustomed to and what has been taught to them. This results in a certain perspective and viewpoint. Everything that they perceive is categorized and evaluated from this concept and form.

Here is a simple example: Researchers look at the animal world and "see" that herds organize themselves in a democratic way. Based on the experience of human beings, the concept is transferred to animals, and people see what they want to see.

Democracy in animals? No such thing. Why should there be! The human eye does not see the energy, cannot hear the communication (the heartbeat), and does not comprehend the true universal signs. Human beings explain the world from their own perspective.

Is this really how it is? My abilities make all of

this visible, and I cannot stop being astonished at what this really involves.

What is the difference between me and being human? I see everything, and human beings see what they want and what they are accustomed to seeing. And I do not mean just me! All those who are awakened perceive things as they really are. This is because they are connected with everything and there is no separation between plant, animal, and being in human manifestation.

My additional task is that I also write, read, and record this information.

Because of their identification, human beings look at the world through the glasses of evaluation and control. They would like to integrate it into their form. This makes the current approach to science and research ridiculous because they see what they want to see instead of opening the perspective so wide that anything is possible. They lack true curiosity, wonder, and the humility to see that this creation is designed in a much more magnificent way than human beings can imagine.

They think that they have subjected the world when they understand and control it, but they do not *see* it. It would be willing to be there for them if they would just look at it and listen.

The eyes offer the essential access for this purpose. Everything can be seen through them, even though this is not about all things coming into consciousness and being given a name.

The prefrontal cortex (an area of the brain that was already described in detail in my book *In the Bliss*) absorbs every type of information. It is located in front of the frontal lobes. This central point sends all of the input information to the heart brain. The latter filters it according to priority and also sends the information to the eye. The inner eye, therefore, receives a huge amount of images, some of which appear visibly before it.

What I consciously perceive with opened eyes is not more than 2 percent of what is there. Everything else takes place through a type of inner world. This is why it is also so easy to read what is going on inside of living beings through their eyes because they reflect their inner states.

Human beings have also introduced restriction and rigidity here. They take the majority of the images from the rational mind and exclude the level of the heart. They believe in what they think they see and make it into their reality again.

If we look at all of this as a type of sequence, it would actually occur as follows: The DNA initially plays the most important role. When it *is* free without the human matrix and activated in its entire length, everything is one, and you will experience yourself being in oneness. The information of the heart brain depends on the genetic code in the DNA. If the DNA is fully activated, your heart brain receives everything what's out there in the universe. Finally, this information is passed on from the heart brain to the eye.

The purer the DNA, the more you awaken and are in the now and the larger your perception, openness, and perspectives becomes.

As a result, you can automatically have a better knowledge of what is true. You will see solutions where there once was a blind spot.

This makes it clearly understandable why the human matrix influences your way of seeing things and prevents you from realizing who you are because this programming only allows a certain radius.

On the other hand, it is wonderful that true seeing has no need to be talked about and noticed. It is simply an openness, an absorbing, allowing the flow, and wonder.

D) Network

Everything is connected with everything else. Everything has the same original source, and everything is pure manifestation from being.

This paragraph actually says it all, which allows you to lean back and *be*.

This could really create much joy, and the creation would be in flow.

But human existence has separated itself from this network. It seems to build its own network, but this has more than one virus in the system.

A main source of disruption is linear thinking. The computer cannot work parallel and multidimensional. It needs inputs from the human hand and a concept because it has no inner world of its own. Expressed in simple terms, it has no DNA and no heart.

This means that such a network idea is simply grotesque and confined in its earliest stages. Instead of "training"—or more precisely, remembering— telepathy, levitation, and being in oneness, you spend an endless amount of time in front of a computer in order to be seen and log yourself into a network.

Will this save humanity? Do Facebook and Twitter help you to know yourself? Do you now know what to do so that you don't walk through life with so much frustration? Have you found a solution for your self-destruction, which you feed every day with your thought patterns and attitudes?

This will not work.

While you sit in front of the computer and input your new experiences so that they are visible and readable by anyone, you will miss out on the present moment. You will not notice the signs of nature and your surrounding world.

This is not directed against the invention of the computer, but it is just an observation about what this platform carries within itself.

Use the natural network—the creation and the almighty power of your being. You can simultaneously experience, communicate, and share everything through it. Everything is connected here through the DNA. The fuel is made of light, and the transporters are certain types of mirror neurons.

What this requires is your pure being and absolute presence. Openness and being awake are then your constant companions. And you will have the experience of such an endless amount of communication that you will be glad to do without the chatter of most human beings.

The network through the computer has not been an acceleration, as it was expected. Instead, it has slowed down the vibrational field of the human matrix immensely. It eats up time without bringing fulfillment because information and communication on the human level contain nothing that connects you with everything. And *everything* is the space within which you move.

The network of the creation matrix is ingenious because it is designed holographically. Everything appears in everything else over and over again. To put this sentence into more understandable terms, a flap of a butterfly's wing on the other side of the planet can trigger a wave. And this is the miracle as well as the power.

The difference to human beings is that the butterfly "knows" about this power because this flap of the wing originates from the true moment.

Human beings create from their artificial rational mind and do not think about the consequences. They believe in a linear concept of time (B follows

A, and C follows B) instead of comprehending that A=B=Z=flower=S=everything.

Wake up and realize who you are. Then your actions will be like the flap of the wing. Everything comes from the moment, from the heart, and from the connection with the DNA.

I act solely from the moment and do not need to think about it. This is not *my* decision or *my* actions. They take place through me. The creation manifests itself through my existence.

Each of us carries this within himself. No one is excluded from this experience. You are the network and simultaneously part of the network. There is no separation and no hierarchy here.

The idea of humanity trying to decide how it will deal with various problems in the future is crazy because there is no future, just now, and this idea assumes that the creation is structured in a linear and static manner.

But I will repeat it one more time: This manifestation is in the endless creative flow of evolution!

Opening up to the moment and your true being are what allows you to continue to exist.

E) Main and Peripheral Setting

Human existence is strange. It has developed something that I call the peripheral setting. When I listen to human beings, I remember that they use their entire strength on dramas and stories that actually happen backstage.

As they do this, they overlook their performance—not to mention the true stage. They are eternally stuck in the scenario that is actually an unimportant one. At the same time, they live in a state of deficit and frustration at not being seen.

It's true that when you spend your entire time behind the curtain and do not simply take the step into the "light," things tend to stay rather dark.

Observe yourself to see how much you blow up the peripheral matters and create soap operas from them instead of picking up the appropriate script.

It is clear that this book would be everything and nothing—empty pages that contain everything, with no instructions as to whether you should enter the stage from the right or the left and, above all, no information about the people and no role into which you should and can slip.

Then it is certainly more comfortable behind the curtain.

When you look at your surrounding world, it will become apparent to you that you spend the majority of your energy on diversions. All of the media aims toward designing the peripheral setting to be interesting and explaining to you that this is actually the essential play. And you take all of this information and circumstances and repeat them either by parroting them or through dramatization. Then the whole thing gets a bit of spice through judgments, and you are already satisfied.

Observe yourself during the course of a day to see how many times you let yourself be led astray and get involved in things that are not important. This is purely a habit and a type of security zone. You are not visible behind the curtain.

The situation is definitely different on the stage. Here, you are present, clear, visible, and acting from the moment. There is no prepared text that you can orient yourself upon, nothing left to hide behind. You also will not need any of this because everything is practically handed to you and you simultaneously become the observer of your performance.

This is where the true life occurs—what is really happening. It is always present without a beginning and without an end.

When you spend a lot of time talking about a certain topic, this is a clear indication that you are staying in the peripheral setting and distracting yourself. Stop your talking, inwardly step out from behind the curtain into the light, and ask yourself the question of what this is really about. Then listen. Be awake and open until you receive a true response. Continue your existence from this point.

Another phenomenon with human beings is their unbelievable power when they can get agitated about something or someone. This releases energy fields that could move mountains. They evaluate and judge and know better. Everyone realizes what I am talking about here. And everyone has made use of this power field because it always takes first place in human existence.

This drama always occurs behind the stage and indicates one of two things: Either this person has something that you also would like to have or he/she mirrors something to you that you also carry within you as a story and an energy field.

Both of these are helpful when you allow yourself

to recognize the drama. And once again, I will make this suggestion to you: Take an exact look, stop your sniveling, become still, step onto the stage, and know yourself. This allows the peripheral setting, which never was there in reality, to come to rest.

And there is one more clarification in relation to the backstage: The more you must speak about your work, your actions, and/or your everyday life, the less clear and happy you are about them. Your self-portrayal is an indication that what you experience is not fulfilling and harmonious for you. And above all, you are once again blowing up the whole thing behind the curtain.

Put yourself on the stage, experience the translation of your heart's desires into reality, awaken, and know who you are. And then you are still. There is no reason to talk extensively about every step that you make, no need for self-portrayal because your being creates itself and manifests on its own. You will be filled with the pure joy of simply being on the stage.

And last but not least, the past and the future are frequently used as peripheral settings. Neither exists on the main stage, but theater is only now, pure and out of the moment.

Human beings catapult themselves out of the now through the stories from back when and how things will be. Both do not exist and no longer exist, and they are just stories. But you are not your story!

Above all, you have felt something and done so through the glasses of the human experience with all of its programs and projections. It has no truthfulness as a result.

What can be so interesting about yesterday and tomorrow when the moment, which now presents itself in such an abundance that it is hardly conceivable, has such magnificence within it.

Leave your stories behind and experience *now* as the main setting.

Humanity has invented something for itself, which is how it destroys itself behind the stage. Its so-called dramas become reality.

Now it is up to you to step out from behind the curtain or simply disappear from the peripheral setting.

Come to the edge.
We could fall down.

Come to the edge.
It is too high!
COME TO THE EDGE.
And they came.
He pushed them,
And they flew.

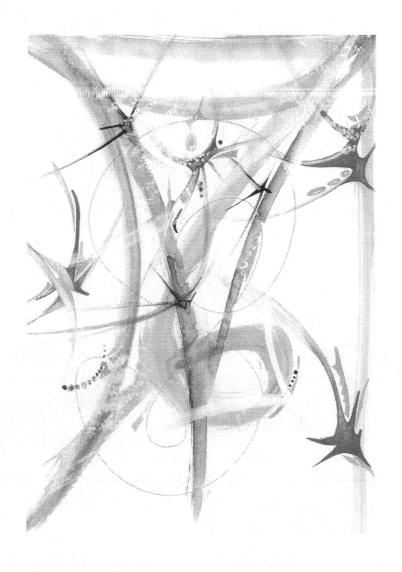

THIRTY-EIGHT
INGREDIENTS OF BEING

Already in my book *In the Bliss,* I could not emphasize often enough that this creation is truly built upon love. Everything is interested in supporting you in your knowing and awakening. Help is offered to you from all sides to remind you of who you really are. Everything wants you to be connected again.

And so it happened that I was shown the substances of the cell fluid. An even better description for them is the ingredients of being that are present in every organism.

The only difference is that they are activated throughout the entire universe but switched off in human beings. This does not mean that they are not there. But they cannot make their contribution.

Why there are exactly thirty-eight is related to a light coding in the ether, but I will write another book to describe this topic in more precise detail.

These ingredients are deactivated because of the human matrix and the pollution of the cell membrane with attitudes, belief systems, and habits. Once you have the experience of enlightenment and are already on the path to removing layer after layer of the human coding, these power fields become active.

This means that you are always the carrier of the almighty and connected with everything. You only need to awaken the almighty from its deep slumber.

This is also why no one can teach you something that you do not already embody. You *are* perfect.

Although I have already published an exercise book for delving more deeply into this activation and resolution, I would like to briefly introduce the thirty-eight ingredients to you here. Even just reading them can awaken something within you. (See *Being Free: 38 Pictures and Exercises to Wake You Up and Set You Free*.)

A) Thirty-Eight Ingredients of Being

1. Magnificence: Words cannot even start to describe the nature of your being. You have a magnificence within you that would like to show itself in everything that is manifested through you.

2. Awareness: Start by surrounding yourself with awareness. Observe your thoughts, feelings, and emotions. Then ask yourself whether they are really yours or not. Awareness leads you into silence. At the same time, you will have a more careful and conscious approach to everything that surrounds you.

3. Presence: Nothing else exists. It is always just *now*. You will be supported in this presence and experience flow if you are truthful.

4. Manifestation: There is no limitation in creating. When you focus on your true being, you materialize it at the same

time. Your almighty being can create everything far more extensively than your human mind can imagine.

5. Silence: When you are in silence and listen to it, everything will be revealed to you. This gives rise to a vastness, joy, and abundance that cannot be expressed with words. You are present in silence.

6. Shining: Light is the platform upon which this creation is based. It wants to flow through all of your cells and bring you to en-*light*-enment. There is pure love in this glow.

7. Being Awakened: You are asleep in a deep trance and not present as a human being. Awaken and know yourself. Being awakened opens your senses and allows you to experience all of the information and the clues that are essential for your fulfilled existence.

8. Abundance: There is no deficit and no suffering. These are human constructs. Being is living in abundance. The creation would like to make the experience that everything—*everything*—is possible

for you. This is about joy and fulfilled being.

9. Trust: You will need trust on your path of self-exploration because everything falls apart. But this trust has a knowledge behind it that you will experience when your true being reveals itself. And the almighty power is in this knowledge.

10. Power: Your being is fed by the almighty power. It can create and heal everything. This should not be compared with human power, which wants to possess and destroy. The power in being penetrates each cell and experiences itself as a type of strength that radiates from within.

11. Laughing: Buddha figures are usually depicted with a smile. Yes, you will be able to laugh heartily about your being when you awaken—above all, what it is not and never was. At the same time, there is such joy that you will have a big grin on your face.

12. Creativity: Your true being has an endless flow of creativity. You experience absolute flow in everything that you

create and do so out of the moment. There is no concept and no instructions here. This arises from within itself.

13. Calmness: Remaining calm is probably one of the greatest challenges. The habit of dramatizing and being angry (at yourself) dominates human existence. Calmness creates space for a new perspective and leads to silence.

14. Beyond Words: Human beings use about 2 to 7 percent of their brains and think that they are completely informed as a result. This is laughable! In your true being, the brain is switched on 100 percent. The entire knowledge is here, and there is simultaneously nothing more to know. Being is beyond words. You can imagine the cleverest ideas about being, and they will not do justice to what you experience.

15. Materialization: One of the greatest miracles is allowing something to become reality. Human beings only use this power within its smallest scope and usually just in terms of possessions. Everything that serves your fulfillment

can be materialized from existence. Your heart's task will be provided with everything that it needs.

16. Joy: Your natural being has pure joy as its basis. The idea of being separate from everything brings the suffering. Instead of just a moment of happiness, this means a joyful being.

17. Fulfillment: Your being is completely fulfilled. Nothing is lacking. As a human being, you are taught that you must do something to change in order to be okay. This is not the truth. Examine all of these instructions and know your true being. You are complete, and everything is within you.

18. Perfection: Being is perfect. It contains beauty, abundance, mercy, and joy. No concept or form exists within it. Only the human matrix declares that something is lacking or should be better. Look at the universe. Isn't this creation unique?

19. Energy: Human beings complain about too little strength and energy. Their identification simultaneously brings

a limitation and, therefore, a deficit. The moment that you *are*, all of the strength is there. It shows you very clearly what is right for you and what is not. Wherever you feel exertion and exhaustion, this is no longer intended for you. Wherever you feel energy and strength, this is your home.

20. Beauty: Nature is the purest beauty, and you have the same quality within you. It is not the concept of the human ideal and form but the way you radiate from within. The joy and love of being can only be reflected through beauty.

21. Mercy: There is a great mercy in knowing your being. Above all, the knowledge and experience of everything and nothing is breathtaking. You will experience every moment as mercy because everything is there and would like to serve you.

22. Devotion: Letting it happen—this is being. Devoting yourself to being in oneness and being open has something wonderful about it. Wanting to possess and wish lists no longer exist because

this arises from itself and shows what should be.

23. Listening: Silence is the key to your true being. You can best listen and clearly receive when your world is still. Being still is truthfulness. You will experience everything that you must know by listening.

24. Almighty: Your true Buddha nature is pure almightiness. You will become aware of this almightiness in knowing your being. There is nothing outside of you. Instead, you *are* almighty.

25. Being: Being requires no words and has no words. It is presence, silence, and being in oneness. It is infinity, joyful, and wonderful! You are not your story because it is just an experience. Your being remains untouched by your story.

26. Freedom: Human beings want to be free and have certain ideas about freedom. A true state of freedom is found in awakening. You no longer cling to anything, and you know about being—that it never ends and has no

beginning. Nothing can happen to you.

27. Truthfulness: You experience no rules or laws in your being, which comes from a true source that flows through you and creates through you. Your speech will change, and your actions will come from the field of joy and love.

28. Dematerialization: Human beings place something in the material world without even having the slightest idea of how to once again dissolve it when it has done its service. Because they do not create from the source of being but from the matrix of human being, huge amounts of waste are produced. Your awareness and your creating are oriented in being so that you can also once again dematerialize these fields and this information.

29. Leisure: The most wonderful way to enjoy your being is in the flow. Even if this sometimes requires effortless discipline, you experience your actions in leisure. No hectic natures and stress

are involved. Leisure is an essential factor that accompanies your being.

30. Infinity: You enter infinity without concepts, belief systems, and principles. Your being is boundless, free, and powerful. Nothing is impossible. There is no limitation on any level. Only the human matrix creates the illusion that you are limited.

31. Clarity: One hundred percent clarity accompanies your awakening. You no longer have any doubt, any chatter in your head, or any questions. Everything that you need is there. Being awakened and clarity are both in your presence.

32. Focus: Human beings are largely without any type of focus. They walk through their lives without a plan and ask themselves why they are so frustrated. They do not take the time to gain clarity and focus for themselves. Your pure being is already focused within itself in connection with everything, and it is awake. Presence does not even allow anything other than this.

33. Knowing: Find out who you really are, and you will experience a deep knowledge. You will know what truthfulness is and how everything is connected. This perception will feel completely natural to you.

34. Courage: You will need courage in your self-exploration—not just in relation to what you will encounter but also toward your surrounding world, which will want to the keep you from your reflection. But courage pays off. Nothing that may manifest has a reality to it. Your true being is free of all these ghosts. Don't forget that you are not your story.

35. Size: Your true size comes from within. You have such power and strength within you. This energy wants to expand and be able to create. It is an expansion on all levels, with joy and love.

36. Humility: Being integrated into the whole allows you to be humble. You will experience the connection to everything that surrounds you in deep

humility. It allows you to become still and be astonished. This is the true creation, and you are a part of it.

37. Thankfulness: Human existence is so busy with its deficits and frustration that it overlooks the miracle and the abundance. Stopping for a moment and being thankful for *being* could change quite a few things. It is not a punishment to be here but a gift to be allowed to have this experience.

38. Miracle: No day passes without miracles. They give being its special magic. But you must open your senses so that you become aware of them. Once you discover them, you will be speechless and live in joy.

B) Activation of the Thirty-Eight Ingredients

What is so different or special about this activation?

When you have the experience of enlightenment, these ingredients are revealed and ready for use. But it is interesting to know that they are not in active use yet.

You could say, "So what? I am free and in being. This doesn't matter." And this is also true. My offer is to go even deeper into this experience of being.

Those who have been awakened are now observers of their manifestation. They are having a human experience without involvement in it, without attachment. They move freely within what is there.

I suggest that you leave behind the perspective that you are having a human experience. Instead, experience the almighty in your being!

Manifest your heart's desire and heart's task, draw from the infinite, and create what wants to appear through you!

This makes a huge difference because it completely eliminates the entire idea of having a body through which you experience your being and various limitations. Then you are no longer an observer of your human idea but pure being in the flow of miracles and magnificence.

Everything is possible!

Don't even try to imagine this because your imagination will only come from the matrix of human consciousness. Being free is not about concepts of this and that.

Instead, the question is whether you dare to "jump" into something that turns all of your preconceived ideas upside down, something that you cannot control and predetermine. Instead, you just devote yourself to it and observe.

You will be integrated into the evolution of this creation with the awakening *and* activation of your ingredients of being.

You can be pure light- and whatever wants to be manifested will appear through you.

This is not a crazy, esoteric idea that I am offering you. You only need to observe the creation and nature. Nothing is fixed. Everything can change in a wonderful way and produce things that are supposedly impossible and eternal.

It is time for you to once again become a part of this and completely say farewell to the concept of the human matrix and being human.

It is worn out and just spinning in its own circles.

This is why it is also destroying itself at the moment, for it cannot exist in separation.

C) Strengthening on All Levels

This world is designed in a holographic way, which means that everything is mirrored in everything else. Here is one example of this: Your total manifestation and entire organism are represented in the cells of your heart. This is why we can probably talk about the heart cell and view it separately in the human concept. But it would simply be stupid to believe that this is just about the heart. Instead, something has become visible in this area that is actually reflected everywhere.

This is an essential factor in your being, namely that you comprehend looking at everything in a holographic way. Nothing is separate unto itself or without a context. Nothing influences just one very specific area and leaves the others untouched.

When you truly allow this to sink into you, then it can be used in an ingenious way and simultaneously in destructive ways, as many examples show.

I would like to remind you of the strength in this creation.

On your path of self-exploration and your awakening, every minute step of discovery and liberation is present and visible in *everything*. You can allow this awareness of yourself to flow into all areas of your life.

The more you depart from the model of lies and recognize that there is no one who suffers or thinks, the more energy will be set free.

It may be that your surrounding world and your remaining rational mind will now want to weaken you (consciously or unconsciously). This weakening is very simple, and it is accomplished through food, clothing, conversation, living, work space, and which decisions you make.

All of these little things are carriers of information. As long as you are not free from the identification of human being and the attachment, they will have their effect on you. In addition, human beings are accustomed to weakening and making themselves small.

When you are exploring yourself, pay attention to your inner voice: What strengthens you in your being What gives you joy and fills you with energy? This has nothing to do with concepts of certain food or clothing. Instead, it is an awakening about how your manifestation can be supported and strengthened. It is a listening, which is essential for you. What would like to be portrayed through your being?

You are completely free in this, without any preconceived ideas. This is more about curiosity and knowing that your true being knows everything, which has a supportive, healing, and strengthening effect on your existence.

It is the experience that everything is there and you don't need to ask anyone.

The beautiful thing about this is that it has no preconceived concepts but is free and flexible within itself.

Take yourself—your almighty being—seriously and listen to how it would like to be strengthened. What feels good to you?

Be awake and aware of what happens in this process. This permeability within and with you will automatically flow into everything because it will be mirrored in the hologram.

SUPPORT

Why does the book include a chapter with this heading? This topic arose from my wealth of experience over the past few months.

You might assume that (as in my other books) suggestions will be provided, but this chapter comes from a very different perspective because I have already offered enough ideas for your self-exploration. The time when you start doing your homework is up to you.

The theme of support has a different background. I held a seminar in California with new people in a new environment as the start of an additional work platform. People offered to support me.

And it did not work—at least not in the way that

they had apparently intended. After I held my seminar, I took a closer look at this "picture." What had happened here? Why could no one translate his/her support into action and make a contribution?

Because they could not provide support for themselves. Human beings are so trapped and limited in their matrix that there is no space for selfless support.

You may now object and claim that things are completely different with you. No, they are not! What human beings can do is to help each other on an external, mostly material level. And some may accomplish a great deal in this respect.

But I am speaking about an inner level of support here—where someone helps carry your energy field, strengthen your matrix, and gives wings to your heart's desire.

As long as you are not free and experiencing yourself and your true being in abundance and joy, no one can support you. This is because you do not even know how support works.

The fields of envy, resentment, and hate get too involved here. This is an essential thing to comprehend: You must first look after yourself and translate your heart's desire into reality. Based on this experience of abundance and joy, you can then unconditionally—*without conditions!*—be there for others.

And if you need support, your creations can help support, promote, and be there for you!

This world does not become a better world through peace movements in resistance to war. This is absurd, and the results speak for themselves. These are beautiful ideas and may set a wave in motion, but they have not reduced the size of the battlegrounds.

First, get to know yourself, leave behind the form of the human being, and allow the creation to become visible through you. This source gives you the powers that you can gladly and easily share with others.

A) Translating Your Heart's Desire into Reality

Take the time—and here I am talking about five to ten minutes—to write down everything that brings you joy.

Read through this list and discover the red thread.

What appears especially often and forces itself into the foreground?

Form one to two words from this and listen to your "field." It is not necessary to do anything with them at first. Just let them sink in and remember. What would happen if you filled your existence with this activity and with this creation? Stop each of these dumb questions: "Yes, but how will this work out? What does this look like? And how will I earn money with it?" This is the human rational mind that immediately gets involved as soon as it sees that you are heading for your true being.

As I already described at the start of this book, each of us in this creation brings a unique package with his contribution to this world. The wonderful thing about this is that none of these are repeated or the same. Even if the words from various people are similar, their creations will ultimately be different.

What stands out to me is that there is not really anything to study or learn in this regard. It comes from your true source. Most of what was taught to you has been stored within yourself more or less successfully as concepts, lies, and false reports.

The majority of this simply has no relevance in

your being. So do *not* be confused if something is on your piece of paper for which you have no training or qualification. This is completely irrelevant.

Your devotion and humility are also essential here. How much can you open yourself and pay attention to the signs for how your heart's desire would like to translate itself into reality? Are you ready for the consequences when you follow it?

Leave behind your human arrogance and comfort in believing that nothing is there, that you see nothing, and that nothing will happen!

This is your little reality that does not correspond with the truth. Then it is better that we do not meet because I can tell you down to the smallest detail about when, how, and where you have received the information and offers. Seeing *everything* is one of my abilities.

But this is not about me. It concerns your being awakened and willing to develop yourself.

It is like the flowers in the field: They grow, blossom, and are simply beautiful now at this moment! And they delight you with their beauty and existence. Now it is your turn to make the flowers happy!

You will receive all of the support that you need. But if this is not possible through human beings, don't lose heart. The universe is not dependent on the human matrix. If this were the case, it would have vanished long ago.

Human beings may help you and give you information, but true support is in everything that surrounds you. The more you have trained to listen and know what strengthens you, the easier it will be for you to recognize the signs. And from the multitude of clues, it will become clear to you what there is to do and which ones will serve you.

On the basis of my own experience, I can only tell you that allowing creativity to flow from and through you—and simultaneously being the observer—is unbelievably enjoyable.

B) Truly Serving

I am no longer important! This is probably one of the most beautiful and touching experiences when you awaken. Your entire ego finally vanishes. The necessity of self-portrayal disappears. What a relief!

So why fulfill a heart's task?

It is your possibility for experiencing that you are almighty. You are a creator, and creation occurs through you. Boundless creativity and love can be manifested and once again dissolved into the entire creation as needed.

You experience joy and serve.

Is it so important to serve?

Yes, everything serves the whole. At the same time, everything is the whole. Yet, your serving is not self-serving but comes from your natural being. This is also the freedom in your creativity because you expect nothing. You also do not compare yourself with others and don't need any encouragement.

Humanity destroying itself is also because human beings do not see any sense in their actions and dealings. They do things because they have been told that they must earn money. Or they refuse to do them because they resist this idea. No matter what side of the coin you serve and support, neither contains any personal responsibility and search for the truth.

The human matrix has the theme of deficit and suffering. This is how people want to be seen, be important, project themselves, and simultaneously (like to) suffer in and because of this unjust, evil world.

Please wake up!

Being is never annihilating! Being is eternal!

Being human annihilates itself. Your being has released itself from *being human*.

You can explore and discover this on your own, or you can allow it to happen.

C) A New World

This creation is new and unique in every moment. Nothing is like it just was. We cannot even comprehend how such an unbelievable experience of evolution and being simply *is*, being constantly in motion and simultaneously in the now, in the moment. I don't even have the words that come close to describing what has been shown to me.

As a human being, you think in the past and in the future. You organize your experiences in sections of time and make predictions as to how things will unfold. But you miss out on the now as you do this. What happened yesterday is completely uninteresting. These are nothing more than stories. It is not being itself.

The creation offers you the opportunity of experiencing yourself *anew* in this world. The new thing about this is your connectedness with everything. It may be presented in a new way for you and simultaneously still be what it always was and always will be.

But what could a world look like if human beings no longer exist and only their manifestations are present in truthful being?

Let us dream … very quietly, in joy and boundless … with no idea! The beautiful thing about this is that being has no concept, no instructions, and no laws. It will be whatever it *is!*

Does it require someone who knows more details? No, it arises from the moment freely and with love.

Do I need to know what will happen tomorrow? It doesn't matter because there is no tomorrow. There is only this moment in which everything is that should be. These questions and a need for answers no longer arise within me because no human being is present. Just because you believe that you see me in a body does not mean that this is the truth. It is the only model that your human matrix allows.

A new world can immediately develop for you when the shell of your identification disappears.

Be astonished about what truly is—everything and nothing!

When you recognize your true being,
Your almightiness,
Then you comprehend this Creation,
And your sense of being separate
disappears.

LIBERATION

A) Mirror

When will you be ready to look in the mirror? How deep must your suffering and misery be before you dare looking at *yourself*?

Or have you already "fallen in love" with what you believe that you see and are?

Do you see what you would like to see and what you believe in?

Self-exploration starts when you take a closer look at the image in the mirror and examine everything that appears before you for its truthfulness.

Do this until nothing more appears because there was also never anything there.

Do you require courage? Oh yes, because all of your excuses and explanations vanish. Things become pure and simple!

Your inside is your outside. What surrounds you is your reality, which becomes visible through your history, belief systems, attitudes, and thoughts.

Suddenly, the separation between you and the rest of the world disappears. You recognize yourself in the mirror: You are this world!

When you dare to explore even further, you will wake up completely. Then this idea of a world and a "you are" also no longer exist. True being is everything and nothing.

Being free is found here—being reflected in the nothing and the everything.

Your person and everything that belongs to it do not even exist. They are only a manifestation from being. This apparent dissolution of the self creates fear from the human standpoint. Your rational mind will give you a thousand reasons why this doesn't work and why it is nonsense.

But who is the rational mind? When you look in the mirror, do you know where exactly it is located and where it manifests itself?

Looking in the mirror means removing your makeup, slipping off your clothes, and undressing your thoughts. Look and explore every word and statement that comes over your lips from all sides to see where they come from and who is even thinking and speaking. Does this sound like work? Yes, this is what I call the homework. But it is worth doing because you are lying to yourself about something in the mirror image that you believe yourself to be.

The idea is not to fall in love with your image like the narcissist or look at it with a special degree of self-hatred.

This is only an appearance with which you are identifying. It is waiting to be uncovered.

As already mentioned above in this book, human beings cling to what they see and want to preserve it.

Use the possibilities of the mirrors to discover your true being in it. It is intended for this purpose.

B) Now

What now? What remains when everything has apparently dissolved? Just the present moment—no more and no less. Yet, whatever must be is suddenly there in your presence. It was just as present before, but your identification kept you so busy that you were not really able to perceive it.

This is also what constitutes the feeling of deficiency, namely being occupied with something that is not even necessary and not wanting to perceive what has priority. There is no one who acts, decides, does, or creates in this process. It happens through you and through this manifestation. The only question is whether or not you will allow to be in the present moment.

There is always just now. Human beings search desperately for the moment and do not even perceive it in this search.

Liberation takes place when you recognize that you are pure being. Human existence is just a taste of many possibilities for how this being manifests its existence. Do not cling to the taste but be open and curious about everything else that awaits you.

The individual components on your journey of discovery to your true being are honesty and truthfulness. When something in your life feels skewed and stressed, then explore to find out the exact reason for this and whether it belongs to you or not. Who is feeling this? What kind of concept is behind it? What happens when you no longer serve it because it is created from an illusion?

Free yourself from serving human laws that say how things must be done and how you must be. Examine all of this for its truthfulness and let it pass by you.

You will be amazed at how much true being shows itself through awareness, love, joy, and being awakened. These come from the source of the almighty and the connection with the entire creation and not just from a construct.

The now offers you the solutions when you listen to and are open for what truly is.

Is there much more to say about this? Words are almost strenuous in this case because they put something into a form and an understanding precisely where this does not exist.

So I will stop and not write anything else about it here. Instead, I invite you into the *now*.

C) Farewell

The decisive "leap" is so difficult for human beings because they must take leave of something. In turn, this arises from the idea that they previously had something that they could cling to.

But being always exists anyway, and the farewell from being human is an illusion. There is nothing that you can lose or leave behind because it has no reality. You have just fallen so much in love with human identification and in whatever it entails that your rational mind explains it as the only truth!

Your self-exploration automatically leads to farewells. When you take off your makeup, your disguise, and your belief systems, you are simultaneously opening yourself to freedom, infiniteness, and magnificence so that you do not just feel a sense of departure. And when you recognize your being, it will no longer exist because everything is always there. Nothing comes and goes!

AWAKENED

I would like to share the image of the swinging door with you in conclusion.

Your human experience looks something like this: There is a type of swinging door that allows manifestation, human existence, and a self to become visible on one side. Then it swings in the other direction, and this is infinity, almightiness, and pure being.

Do you remain in the space of manifestation and claim, "This is all that can be experienced here?" If so, consider this back and forth from the perspective of infinity and let yourself be surprised by what is concealed behind it the next time that the door swings open.

Awakening means knowing about this door and being with it. But there is no attachment that is concealed behind it. There is no expectation about what should and must appear, so be amazed and let yourself be surprised.

In closing, I would like to tell you a story from the Indian master Papanjali: Once upon a time, there was an old king. His wife had already died, and he had no successor. He wanted to retire, so he had an announcement made throughout the country that the appropriate candidates should apply for the position of king.

Thousands of people, both old and young, showed up at his door.

Then they were first required to pass a type of test for six months before they would be invited to a conversation with the king.

They were asked to experience everything related to the position of king:

1. The royal bath
2. Clothing and jewelry
3. Riding horses
4. Politics
5. Meditation

A week before the conclusion of this testing

period, the king sent his ministers to check on how the applicants were faring.

The ministers entered the royal bath. It was overflowing with people who were now engaged in lively business transactions. In response to the question of why they were still there, they gave this answer: "We will stay here. Give our best regards to the king, but we already have a business with Reiki and massages and bath treatments. Please give the king our business cards because he is warmly invited to see us."

Then the ministers went into the second room. This was also filled with people who were dressed in the most beautiful clothing and who wore and passed around the jewelry. "What are you doing there? You should already be passing the other tests," said the ministers.

But here as well, the people told them that they were already involved in business transactions and everyone was selling, offering, and marketing something.

It was no different with the horses. The people also wanted to stay there and engage in their business deals, but they said that the king was welcome to make use of their services.

CONCLUSION

Everything that has been written here and continually repeated in part is not addressed to your person.

Instead, it serves to speak to your awareness so that it remembers its true being.

When you make the decision *to jump*, it is not as a human being. Instead, your awareness has the gift of taking a closer look at your enactment and getting to know it.

And now? It's your turn—everything is ready!

In the area of politics, groups had formed. The people had lively discussions with each other and talked like they were quite important. They offered to gladly share a few of their ideas with the ministers, but they definitely want to stay where they were.

Then the ministers came to the last room—the temple. And it was empty.

They returned to the king and gave him a report about their excursion.

He was taken aback and asked, "Was no one in the sacred room?"

So they told him that there was just a twelve-year-old boy who spent his time there and cleaned it.

"Bring me this boy," said the king.

When the boy was brought to him, the king asked, "What are you doing in my temple?"

"I have cleaned this room ever since I was a small child."

"Why have I never seen you?" asked the king.

"I always hide when your highness comes. I see that the king finds pleasure in all of the other things, but he is untouched by them in this temple.

None of this is important here. In addition to removing your clothing, you also set aside all of your thoughts. This is my favorite place!"

In response, the king said, "Only this boy is suitable."